PIECES OF ME

How Fate Brought Me Home

STEPHEN CASTRO

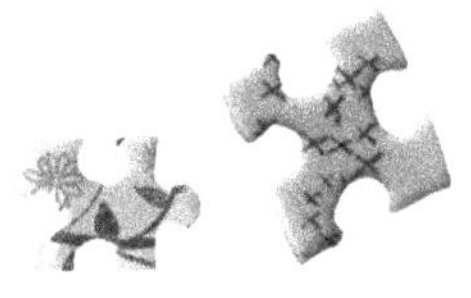

"You have the power to alchemize your reality."

Stephen Castro

Contents

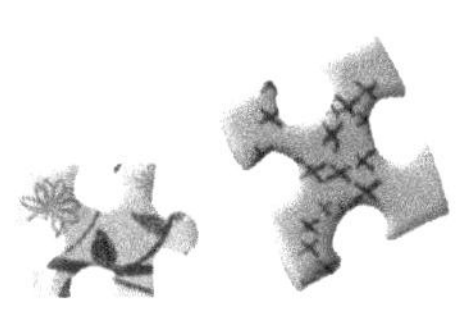

Preface

One week in May, we were doing a Saturday cleaning. I was cleaning the top shelf of my closet, when a journal fell down and hit me right in the head.

I opened it and began to read.

"The first day of Catholic school, when I made a joke in class, Sister Anna smacked my hand so hard with the ruler for disturbing the class. I began to feel the warm sensation of pee drizzle down my leg. That was my first memory of school."

My father had begun to write his life story.

This made me think about how I would start my own story. Maybe something that catches the attention of the reader, like:

It was the hottest day of the year, a scorching inferno that seemed to consume everything in its path. The sun beat down relentlessly, baking the pavement and turning the air into a stifling haze. Some say it was so hot because the gates of hell had opened, releasing a baby who came screaming into the world. Others said that it was just the dog days of August. That day in August a baby was born and that baby was me. Now as to how I was created ...

Sadly, my father never did finish writing his life story. Part of the reason I choose to share my life today is to honor his memory and try to finish one of his dreams that he ran out of time to complete.

When my parents moved into their first apartment together after I was born, they put together a jigsaw puzzle of a home sweet home welcome mat and framed it. They hung it in our living room. That was in 1978. Today I sit on my back porch and still gaze upon the same picture in the same frame. It puts a grin on my face as I reminisce and reflect on how we are all made up of moments in our life that have all had major effects on who we are.

Like a puzzle, each interaction is a different puzzle piece that we try to fit into who we are or who we want to be. How we talk, walk, think, react, and interact with the world around us. From the first time that we take a breath we are growing, learning, and building our puzzle. We are becoming the human that we want to be with every new interaction we experience and every emotion that we can associate with the experience, both good and bad.

When we experience a trauma in our lives, it breaks the puzzle and we fall to pieces. Our job is to pick up the pieces and put the pieces together and make the connections to put the pieces together. You will find new pieces that fit, because your puzzle gets changed.

When the puzzle falls to pieces and we pick it up and try to put it back together, the trauma changes the shape of some of the pieces, which is why the puzzle fell apart in the first place.

When we try to hold onto the old picture of who we were before the trauma, the puzzle never quite fits right again because it's not meant to fit the same anymore. You are not the same person as you were before you experienced the trauma. The puzzle is incomplete after, but that is OK because we have to find new pieces that fit. Some might fit for a little while and fall off and some might fit forever.

It is up to us to find these pieces that fit and **we find them by living life again.** The secret is that the puzzle is made to be easily taken apart and put back together so that we can shape our puzzle in any way we see fit to live our life.

We are always whole, and the universe is always working for us, when we are doing what we are supposed to be doing. Once you know that, you can trust that the universe will be working for us. That gives us the power to alchemize our reality!

You might not find all the pieces fit, but eventually you figure out which ones do. The more people that you connect with, the quicker you will fix your puzzle and bring the pieces back together. But if we stay scared, and try to put the pieces together on your own, it could be years with the puzzle being incomplete and having that empty feeling inside. So I say keep living and keep building your puzzle. Why stop at a 100 piece puzzle when we can be a 10,000 piece puzzle?

This book is the story of the pieces that make up me.

Chapter One

02 13 14 12 12

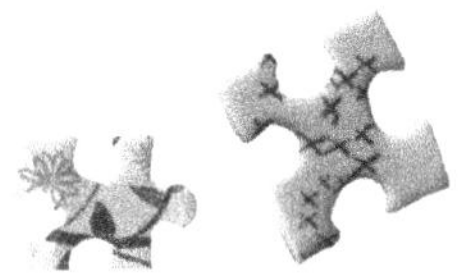

Tic ... toc ... In the stark, white room, the rhythmic sound of the clock ticking filled the air, amplifying the sense of anticipation. Each tick seemed to echo louder than the last, reverberating through the sterile space. The room was filled with a multitude of medical staff, their faces masked with focus, their anticipation tangible as they awaited the directive of the lead doctor to commence the procedure.

Amid the hum of machines and the hushed whispers of staff, I sat at my wife's bedside, my hand intertwined with hers as she lay sleeping, her expression serene despite the gravity of the situation. My mind, however, was far from serene. The ticking of the clock seemed to reverberate in my head, intensifying the knot of anxiety coiled in my chest.

As I sat there, I found myself drifting into a contemplative state, my thoughts meandering the corridors of my mind. They say that the sons pay for the sins of their fathers, a notion that had often haunted me in quiet moments. I remembered my father and how the weight of his transgressions haunted him, casting long shadows over his existence.

I carry my father's name, a burden that felt heavier in moments like these. Did the sins of the past inevitably seep into the present, shaping the destiny of the future generations? Did I, too, unknowingly set a course for my son, my namesake, to navigate a similar tumultuous path?

My mind spiraled, grappling with a whirlwind of emotions and doubts. My thoughts were a tempestuous sea churning with regrets and fears. I pondered the choices I had made, the mistakes I had committed, and wondered how they would echo through the generations to come.

Lost in the labyrinth of my thoughts, I barely registered the precise moment when the lead doctor, with a decisive gesture, signaled the start of the procedure. My heart pounded in my chest, the ticking of the clock seeming to meld with the erratic rhythm of my pulse.

As the incision was made, the room seemed to hold its breath, collective focus zeroed in on the pivotal moment unfolding. Time blurred, warped by the intensity of the moment until, at exactly 12:12 p.m. on the 13th of February, 2014, a wail pierced the air, breaking the tension like a crescendo.

My eyes widened as my son made his grand entrance into the world—a tiny, miraculous being announcing his arrival with fervor. My newborn son thrashed around peeing everywhere and cried, a jubilant proclamation of his existence, of his resilience in the face of adversity.

Through tears of relief and overwhelming joy, I gazed upon my son, who seemed to defy all odds with his fiery spirit. In that moment, amidst the chaos and jubilation, a sense of profound gratitude washed over me, a realization that my son was a testament to the strength and resilience that coursed through our bloodline.

My son's cries echoed like a declaration of defiance, a proclamation that he had weathered the storm of birth to claim his place in the world. He was a fighter, a warrior born into a lineage marked by hardships and trials.

Yet, as swiftly as the moment arrived, it was snatched away. My baby boy was whisked off to the Intensive Care Unit for further observation and care. He was born at 32 weeks and weighed one pound, six ounces. My heart twisted with worry, a thread of fear weaving through the fabric of my elation.

As I stood there, grappling with the whirlwind of emotions that threatened to overwhelm me, I knew one thing for certain: that moment, the birth of my son, marked a turning point, a crossroads from which my life would never be the same.

As I watched the medical staff hurry away with my son, a sense of profound responsibility settled over me, a fierce determination to protect and nurture the fragile life that now rested in my hands. The clock continued its relentless journey, ticking ever onward, a reminder of the inexorable passage of time and the uncertain road that lay ahead.

In that moment of stillness and chaos, of joy and fear intertwined, a new chapter unfurled before me. It beckoned me to embark on a journey filled with uncertainties, challenges, and boundless love. As I stood there, gazing into the unknown horizon, I knew that my life had been irrevocably altered, transformed by the arrival of my son, a beacon of hope in a world fraught with shadows.

How did we get here? I wondered. Perhaps it was fate, or perhaps it was simply the relentless march of time, carrying us forward into uncharted waters. I took a deep breath, steadying myself for the road ahead. I knew that whatever trials lay in store, I would face them with unwavering determination, guided by the love that now bound me to my son, my flesh and blood, my legacy.

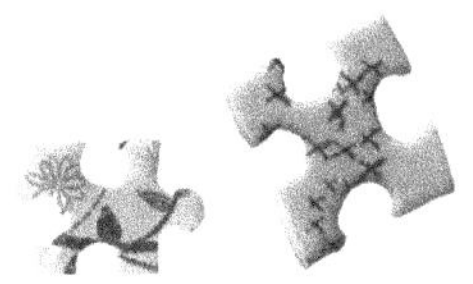

Chapter Two

My Parents

My parents were young and filled with dreams when they met. My mother, just eighteen at the time, had dropped out of school to pursue a career in fashion design. My mother had a stunning body to go along with her gorgeous looks. The nickname she was known by was "Boobie" for all the obvious reasons. She had caught the eye of *Playboy* magazine, which was eager to feature her in its pages.

My father, a few years older, had been a star athlete in school, excelling in both basketball and baseball. After leaving school, he had found himself aimlessly hanging out with friends in the projects of the big city.

It was during this time that fate intervened, as my parents met while hanging out with their respective friends. Their connection was instant and undeniable. A year later, the two of them had been dating exclusively and were very serious about each other; they were married, and a few weeks after that, I was born. I know, you do the math, did they get married for love or for the baby that was baking in the oven? The traditional way of life wasn't in the cards for my family at any time in our lives.

I wasn't the best behaved child. One time I had turned on the gas stove and went to my room. When my mother went to light the stove to start cooking, it blew up. She was burned. We were lucky that she wasn't hurt badly.

Keeping my parents on their toes wasn't enough. The next few years were marked by a series of heartaches, as my parents experienced multiple miscarriages. Finally, their perseverance paid off, and my brother was born. And then, after one last tragedy, my baby sister completed our family.

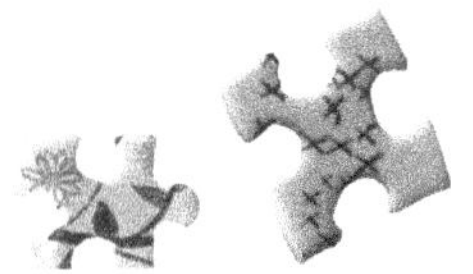

Chapter Three
Heroin's Grip

It was the 80s, and the city was in the grip of a devastating epidemic. The Big H, dope, Black Tar, or Mexican Brown, better known as heroin, had become the drug of choice, ravaging the lives of its users with its addictive grip. The city streets resembled a post-apocalyptic wasteland, as people succumbed to its power, seeking solace from the pain and problems of life.

Unfortunately, my mother and father were not exempt from its temptations. Before long, heroin had consumed their lives, and all they could do was chase that high, constantly searching for the next hit to forget their troubles and briefly feel good again. Nothing ever feels as good as the first time.

I was only four or five years old when I began to realize the magnitude of their struggle. I would stand outside the bathroom, banging on the door, tearfully pleading for my parents to come out. But they were trapped inside, lost in a haze of heroin. Something had to change. They knew they needed help, but they didn't know how to break free from the clutches of addiction.

During the day while my mom was doing the day-to-day duties of a stay-at-home wife, I would go to the living room and turn on the television and put on *The 700 Club. The 700 Club* was a show hosted by Jimmy Graham, a very popular preacher. After turning on the TV, I would leave the room and go back to playing in my room. When my mother would turn it off, I would run back into the room and turn it back on and tell her that I was watching the show. This would go on and on. That show was my mom's first real introduction to religion. I can't say exactly why I would keep wanting to have the show on while I was playing in my room. Maybe I liked the background noise, maybe there was a voice in my head telling me that this is what my mother needed to hear so I must help her listen.

After failed attempts at detox day clinics, fate stepped in once again. My parents discovered a program located in upstate New York, in the mountain forest far from the chaos of the city. This program offered individual and, eventually, family rehabilitation. They made the difficult decision to enter the program. I was placed in my grandmother's care, my brother stayed with a third cousin, and my sister stayed with our aunt.

My parents embarked on their journey to recovery.

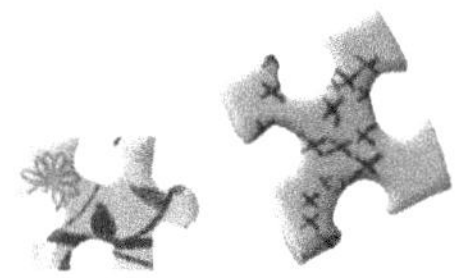

Chapter Four

Living with Grandma

Living with my grandmother was bittersweet. She was one of the toughest women I knew. She was French and her family disowned her when she married a Puerto Rican man. They had six kids—four girls and two boys. She had to always do everything on her own, without her family.

When I went to live with her, she was in the early stages of arthritis, which would eventually leave her bedridden until her passing.

Most of the time I was out playing in the big playground of the city. At the time, people would just hang out in the streets, in the basements and the front stoops of the apartment buildings that made up the projects. People would be playing music from their boomboxes. In the summer, fire hydrants were opened so kids and adults alike could cool off from the hot sun's rays. The girls played jump rope and Double Dutch. The boys played tag, kick the can, leapfrog, stickball, and hide-and-go-seek.

This one time I was playing tag and I was it. I was chasing my friend around the apartment buildings trying to tag him. My friend ran into my building, slamming the door behind him to try to hinder my progress to tag him.

As I ran up to the door, it was closing. I put my arm out to stop the door and my hand went through the glass window in the door. There was a loud shatter and glass was everywhere. I was frozen for a split second and so was my friend.

We quickly realized that somehow I wasn't hurt. There was not even a scratch! We continued to run and play. Later my grandma hit me with her slipper on my butt, and punished me for breaking the door. She said I was lucky I didn't get hurt.

Although her condition limited her mobility, she provided me with love and stability during those uncertain times.

Meanwhile, my brother found solace with our third cousin. She had no kids so he was treated as if he was her own son.

My baby sister stayed with our aunt who had two boys of her own so my sister was like a daughter to her family.

The separation was painful, but it was necessary for our family's healing.

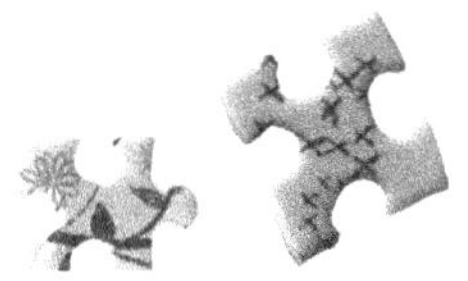

Chapter Five

Family Recovery

Months turned into a year, as my parents fought their battles separately. Eventually, they conquered their demons, obtaining their GEDs, and successfully completing their rehabilitation.

We were finally able to reunite as a family, and we were granted the chance to begin anew in a serene and peaceful setting upstate.

First, my parents were there alone together. Then, a few months later, I was sent to live with them. A few more months later, my brother came, and finally my sister was brought up to join us. We were all together for the first time in almost two years.

Our new home was a cozy cabin nestled among towering trees and surrounded by a pristine lake. The air was fresh and untainted, free from the pollution of the city. We fished, swam, and played without a care in the world, reveling in the joy of being together. For a while, it truly felt like we had found our own little paradise. The noises of the city were replaced by the noises of the forest. The sounds of different animals and insects all day and night echoed throughout the trees in the woods.

This paradise, however, was not without drama. One time during the winter we were all outside playing in the snow and I was throwing what I thought was a snowball at my brother. It turned out to be a rock covered in snow!

Needless to say, when it hit him in the forehead, it cracked open a big gash and blood started to leak down his face.

I saw his blood-covered face and heard my mother's voice scream, *"I am going to kill you, what did you do to your brother?"*

My fear kicked in and I ran inside the house and hid under my bed. My parents gave chase, trying to pull me out from under the bed, but I was holding onto the frame of the bed for dear life. They tried to use a broom and poke me out from under the bed again. I wasn't budging. They moved the bed and I just moved with it. I don't think I came out for two days. I was so scared. The wound healed. It left a nice scar right in the middle of his forehead.

Getting through family issues like that was what we had to learn together. Just like the wound healed, so did our family.

Graduation from the family rehab program loomed on the horizon, forcing my parents to face a difficult decision. Should they return to the city, where temptations lurked around every corner, knowing that the poisonous grip of addiction could easily resurface? In the end, they knew what was best for our family's future. They chose to leave behind everything they had known, turning their backs on the city and all its temptations. We moved to West Hartford, Connecticut. Out new home was only a few hours from the city, but it felt like we had entered another world.

We began forging a path filled with hope and resilience. The road ahead would be tough, but our family was stronger than ever. Together, we had overcome great adversity, and in that transformation, we found something truly remarkable—the power to create our own destiny.

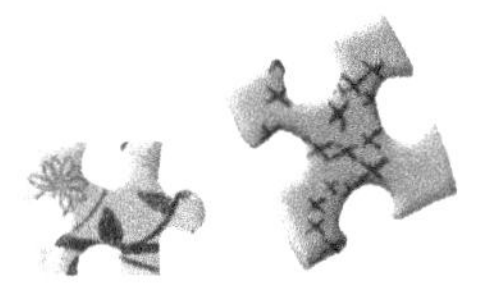

Chapter Six

New Beginnings in a New State

Moving to another state was just the beginning of our problems. Even though it was only a few hours away, it seemed like we were a million miles away from all the sins of the city that we were running away from.

It was fall and the trees were all turning beautiful colors. It made for a beautiful backdrop to our struggles that laid ahead. We had no place to live and very little clothes and belongings. The only possessions we carried with us were our dreams and hope for a better future. It was a tough start, but we refused to give up.

After days of searching, we stumbled across a small apartment above a liquor store, nestled next to a tattoo parlor. It wasn't luxurious by any means, but it was a shelter. The scent of alcohol mingled with the ink in the air, creating a unique atmosphere that would become our home.

It was also a hard adjustment to the different sounds at night. In New York City, people screaming and fighting, sirens blaring through the night, trains running all night long, cab horns sounding every 20 minutes like clockwork were the soothing sounds that would put me to sleep. Living in the woods as we had while at family rehab, while sounding very different, hadn't been so quiet either. There were all types of animal noises that made it loud enough to rest. Being in West Hartford, all those sounds at night weren't present. It made me toss and turn most nights. Decades later, I am still not used to the silence of the smaller city we live in today.

My father, armed with his GED, secured a job as an exterminator. Back in those days, the job description consisted of bombing sites with smoke and then courageously facing the rats with bats as they scurried out of buildings, beating them to death, then disposing of the rodents. It was a grim task, but my father never wavered in his determination to provide for us. Meanwhile, my mother embraced her role as a stay-at-home wife, diligently taking care of me, my brother, and baby sister.

As for me, I was on the verge of embarking on my first-ever school experience. Although my age qualified me for first grade, the school felt it best if I started in kindergarten, considering my lack of prior education.

It was a new chapter, filled with apprehension and excitement. I was bigger than most of the kids in my class since I was supposed to be in the next grade above me. I had my share of fights and acting-out behavior being that I was the new kid in a new town.

It was a hard adjustment for me. I remember giving one kid a bloody nose at recess when he wouldn't leave me alone.

Another time I threw a chair at a teacher in class and ran away from the school. I had a rough journey to say the least.

What finally helped me to turn around my behaviors was finding sports. In order to play sports in school, I had to get good grades and have good behavior, so I started to turn things around.

To aid my parents in their journey towards recovery, the family rehab program connected us with a local church. This newly-formed church was affiliated with the program that had helped us. From that point on, if we weren't at school or work, we were at church. It became a central part of our lives, providing the structure and support that my parents desperately needed.

Every Tuesday night, from 7:30 p.m. to 10 p.m., we gathered for church service. Wednesdays were filled with choir practice from 6 p.m. to 8 p.m., and Thursdays were dedicated to engaging bible study sessions from 7 p.m. to 9 p.m. As the weekend approached, we eagerly anticipated Friday night church services that lasted until 11 p.m. Afterwards, we would gather in the back of the church, sharing food and fellowship that often lasted until the early hours of the morning.

Saturdays were dedicated to ministering to the people of the city, with my parents leading the way. As children, we often trailed along, feeling the weight of the responsibility without fully understanding it. My parents would take us to some of the worst neighborhoods in town. They were drug infested, with used syringes and other paraphernalia scattered everywhere. You could find violence around any corner, but these were the places that needed the most attention in their mind for lives that the Lord could save with their help.

These days were not the most enjoyable for us, but we knew it was part of the journey our family was undertaking. My parents would be singing church hymns and passing out flyers, as well as speaking to people about what God had been doing in their lives. We just sort of stayed close by and played with each other and the local kids that were gathering around when the singing started.

The marathon of Sundays greeted us with services starting at 11 a.m. and stretching until 7:30 p.m. Sunday school would start at 11 a.m. and go on for what seemed like hours. At 1 p.m., the service would start with worship of singing and testimony from the congregation and ending in prayer. Some Sundays we wouldn't leave until after 8 p.m.

As a child, these endless Sundays felt like torture. The hours dragged on, testing my endurance and patience. Nevertheless, it was all a part of the structure and support system that kept our family grounded and focused on a better life.

After a while, things did start to improve. Just as the church grew, so did my parents. They began leading a couple's sub-ministry, catering to married couples who were walking in faith. As their personal growth flourished, so did their professional endeavors. My mother pursued a career with her GED, expanding her opportunities for employment. Meanwhile, my father, fueled by his unwavering work ethic, got a job working for the electric company starting at the bottom. He transitioned from being a meter reader for the light company to becoming a skilled lineman, working on electric wires and poles.

I recall nights when my father would come home, silently yearning for hurricanes or inclement weather to strike. The overtime work that such weather brought would help provide better for our family.

One day in 1992, a big hurricane hit our town. It blew the doors off of the apartment and left destruction in its path wherever it went. My father was so happy to be out working during this storm making overtime and hazard pay to keep people's lights and power on during the storm. It was in these small moments of sacrifice and dedication that I witnessed my parents' unwavering love and commitment to our well-being.

Slowly but surely, our circumstances began to change. We became a united family, with my siblings and I attending school while my father took on a good job with great benefits. With my parents' roles expanding within the church and their personal growth, our lives transformed. We finally had the stability, security, and happiness we had longed for.

Moving to a new state had initially posed a series of challenges and obstacles, but it also ignited the flame of resilience within our family. We fought against adversity, supported each other through hardships, and with the help of the church, transformed our lives for the better.

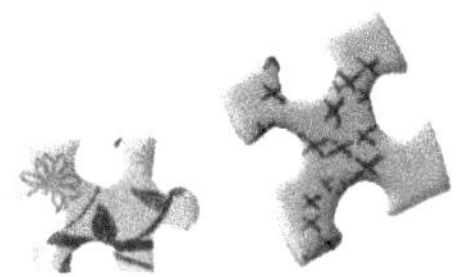

Chapter Seven

Dreams

As the sun rose high in the sky, casting a golden hue over the small town, life seemed to be filled with dreams and possibilities. It was 1991. I was 11 years old. We were settling into our new house, a humble abode that my parents had worked relentlessly to provide for us. It was only the next town over to Hartford and was our third place that we had moved to in the last few years.

My parents had rented our first two houses, all the while working towards buying and owning a house of their own. This new house promised a backyard and individual bedrooms, more than one bathroom, and even an above ground pool—something we had always longed for. Every person's dream that lived in the projects was to own their own house with a yard, a fence, and a dog. My parents had achieved that dream for us!

Little did we know that our lives were about to take an unexpected turn, one that would shatter our dreams and change us forever.

One fateful day, as the air crackled with anticipation, my father embarked on a routine task. He was helping change an electrical pole, his strong hands guiding the new pole off the truck. But then, with a horrifying snap, the straps broke, and the heavy pole plummeted towards the ground, splat like a watermelon that fell to the ground. My dad's leg was crushed to mush. Time seemed to slow down as the realization hit me: my father was caught under the weight of 2,000 pounds, his leg bearing the brunt of the impact from over a four-feet fall.

The hospital became our second home as my father fought for his life not knowing if he would lose his leg. I remember visiting him and seeing his leg wrapped in a labyrinth of poles and bolts, as if a construction site had taken residence within him. The doctors skillfully pieced his shattered leg back together, saving it from certain amputation. Hope flickered in our hearts, as we believed that soon my father would regain his strength and be back to work, providing for our family once again.

But life had other plans for us. The routine follow-up appointment after the accident took an unexpected turn. The doctor's words reverberated through the sterile walls, chilling our bones and shattering our existence. My father's blood work had come back positive for HIV.

In those days, information about the virus was scant, and fear gripped our souls as we faced the daunting task of getting tested ourselves. I was eleven, my brother was eight, and my sister was six. It was a cruel test of innocence that children should never have to endure.

When the test results arrived, our lives cascaded into a whirlpool of emotions. My mother, father, and little sister were all positive, while my brother and I remained negative. Questions haunted us: why had such a cruel fate befallen our family? Follow-ups and medications became part of our daily routine, punctuated by the numbing sense of loss and uncertainty.

After finding out the devastating news about my family's future, my little sister was put into the Make-A-Wish Foundation program. They make a wish come true for children with terminal sickness. My sister wanted to meet her favorite music group New Kids On The Block. My father had another block that he wanted for us. We headed to Disney World! The happiest place on earth! He wanted us to check off another number off the list of dreams to accomplish with your family.

We had two weeks of fun in the sun and riding all the rides in all the amusement parks. The Make-A-Wish team paid for the whole thing including giving us passes to all the parks. We had food vouchers and even had a cut-the-line pass to ride all the rides and not wait in line. Some of the lines were over an hour long, and in the heat, so waiting would have been unbearable. Not for us, though. We would show the pass and get escorted to the front of the line. For some rides, we would get to go inside the rides building into a VIP area with food and air conditioning. They would stop the ride and let us in on some real VIP treatment. The two weeks went by so fast and with freshman year around the corner, it was time to get back home and prepare.

Once home, my father's faith, once unwavering, crumbled under the weight of despair. He retreated from the church and lost himself. The division between my parents became a fault line in our family. As children, we were forced to choose sides, tearing our home apart with unease and conflict.

I don't blame my father for how he reacted to the situation, learning that the actions he took in his youth would have such drastic consequences on his family in the future. Once he made the decision to change his and my mother's life for the better, all he did was sacrifice for his family till his end. I will always keep his work ethic and drive with me throughout all the years of my life.

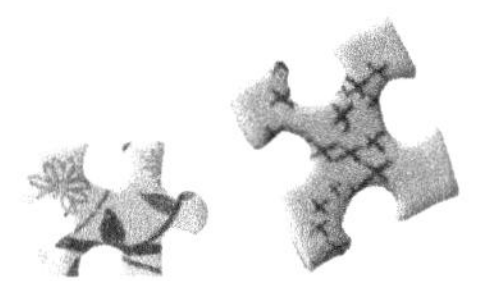

Chapter Eight
Man of the House

A new chapter began. The year was now 1993. I entered high school, transitioning from the familiar comfort of elementary and middle school to a vast sea of 1,000 students in my freshman class. Of the 1,000 students, less than 250 students graduated. The adjustment to high school was overwhelming.

Life had a way of throwing curveballs that even the strongest hearts struggled to handle. In November, while sitting in class, I was abruptly summoned by my guidance counselor. Her eyes held a sorrowful weight as she gently broke the news—my father had passed away, succumbing to AIDS.

When we had visited him the weekend before, I had a feeling that his days would be coming to an end soon. He couldn't form sentences. When he spoke, it was just a few words mixed in with gibberish, almost childlike. So I wasn't thrown for a loop, but I was still devastated.

At that moment, as a thirteen-year-old boy, I was thrust into the role of being the man of the house. At the same time I was going through puberty, becoming a man, and starting my freshman year of high school.

I was navigating my own journey, trying to find my place in this world, but suddenly, I was called up to the big leagues. I wasn't ready, and the weight of responsibility threatened to crush me. The transition to high school, already tumultuous, now carried the gargantuan burden of loss and the need to carry on.

My mother was now a single mom with three kids trying to survive. She turned to the church for support through the tough times.

As the oldest, I had to be the moral support and pick up the slack at home. I took on more responsibilities within the house. I had to help cook and help do the day-to-day house chores that my mother would normally do. Now that she had to work two jobs it fell on me to get it done.

My mother tried her best to keep a smile on her face and stay strong during all of the struggles we were dealing with. It took a lot out of her. She was now both our mother and our father. In one swift moment, my mom put on all the hats in the world to keep her family together. She took everything she had left inside and turned it all into making the best life for her family. My mom didn't even entertain another relationship with a man. Even though I could tell she was feeling lonely, she never complained or took anything out on us kids.

I have to give her all the credit. She just did what had to be done without hesitating. It stayed with me like a branding etched in my skin that the power of love can give you the strength to make any change you need.

Even with a blur of emotions and uncertainty clouding every step, I somehow managed to survive my freshman year. But as I entered my sophomore year, another life-changing chapter unfolded before me, one that would shape the man I would become.

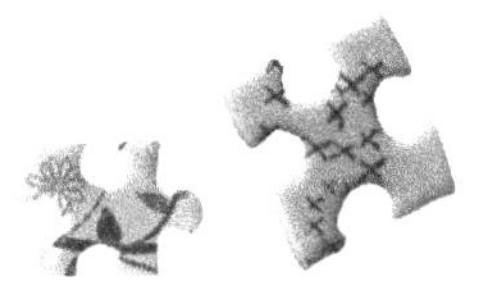

Chapter Nine

A Twist of Fate

My sophomore year of high school will be forever etched in my memory. It was during that year that I encountered the most remarkable person who would eventually be a big puzzle piece for me—my special friend. However, the path to our love story was anything but easy.

During my freshman year, our paths never crossed. It seemed as if our lives were running parallel, going in completely different directions. But fate had something else in store for us. As sophomore year began, we found ourselves in an astonishing twist of fate, sharing five out of our eight periods together.

The first time I laid eyes on her, I was captivated by her beauty, humor, and caring nature. She possessed a strength that shone through her involvement in the varsity soccer team. I couldn't help but be drawn to her. Every day, I found myself sitting behind her in class, engaging in effortless conversations. Sometimes, I would playfully run my fingers through her hair, cherishing those moments until the bell rang.

Though our interactions were limited to the classroom, the winter break provided the perfect opportunity for me to reach out to her. With a heart pounding like a thousand butterflies, I handed her a letter with my phone number in the stairwell before she left for home on a Friday. Her warmth and laughter echoed in my mind, but doubts crept in, questioning whether she would actually call.

To my amazement, she did call that same night, and we embarked on an exhilarating conversation that lasted from 8 p.m. to 6 a.m. There was never a moment of silence or a pause; our connection flowed effortlessly. Throughout the break, we spoke to each other almost every day, for hours on end. We never ran out of things to say, immersing ourselves in each other's thoughts and ideas, only pausing when she had to lower her voice to avoid waking her grandmother.

I learned more about her life, her family, and the unique structure of her home. She lived in a three-family house, with her uncle residing on the third floor, her parents and siblings on the second floor, and she occupied the first floor with her beloved grandmother. These conversations deepened our bond, and I found myself falling head over heels for her.

The only obstacle that stood between us was the fact that she was in a relationship with an older guy, and they seemed serious. Despite this, my feelings for her consumed me, and I felt compelled to confess. One day, she walked me home from school, a journey spanning over two miles. We spent time at my house, accompanied by her cousin. It was the perfect opportunity to reveal my true feelings.

As I showed her around my house, the tour ended in my basement. In a moment of boldness and overwhelming emotions, I kissed her. It was a magical, unforgettable moment that transported me to the heavens.

They left shortly after, and we continued our usual nightly phone conversations. Spring was approaching, and now that she knew how I felt, we shared dreams of a future together, contemplating what our children might look like. I basked in the belief that she saw me as the perfect boyfriend. She stated several times that if she didn't have a boyfriend I would be the perfect man to be with.

Things grew complicated as her relationship began to crumble. The day finally arrived when she broke up with her boyfriend, and I rejoiced, convinced that our time to be together had finally come. But, fate once again intervened, and she disclosed that she needed time and space to clear her mind. Disheartened, I reluctantly accepted her decision, believing that we would eventually be reunited.

Unfortunately, three weeks later, my world collapsed. She started dating a senior on the football team, and the pain I experienced was indescribable. I found myself utterly shattered, my heart broken into a thousand pieces. I cried incessantly for four days, unable to comprehend how someone who made me feel so good could inflict such deep pain. Our connection severed, and I couldn't bear to look at her or speak to her. Silence became our vocabulary for the remainder of the school year.

My sophomore year will always hold a special place in my heart, defined by a tale of hope, love, and heartbreak. The memories of our time together were bittersweet reminders of what once was, leaving a scar that may take a lifetime to heal. But perhaps, just maybe, with time, fate would intervene again, granting us a second chance to create yet another remarkable chapter in our lives.

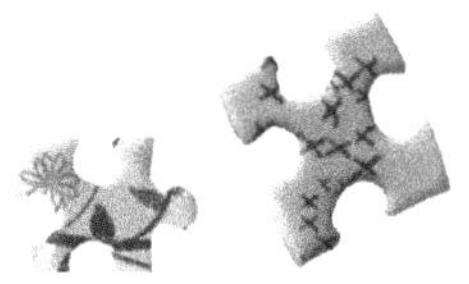

Chapter Ten
Moving into Junior Year

As the summer days melted away, anxiety bubbled within me as I watched the arrival of my junior year. The past year had separated my special friend and me, leaving a gaping hole within my heart and a quiet void that once held our conversations. We no longer spoke, drifting apart like broken pieces of a jigsaw puzzle. It was easier to avoid her during our junior year, as fate dictated that we had no classes together, unlike the torment of our sophomore year.

To help keep my mind from dwelling on my lost love I went out and got a job working after school with elementary school kids from the projects. We would help them with their schoolwork, provide after school snacks and, in the summer months, breakfast and lunch for those whose parents were always away working. We were like mentors to them also. The pay wasn't great but it kept me busy and the joy of helping the children was fulfilling.

It also kept me away from home. My mother was trying her best to be a mom and a dad but it was hard. Disciplining my siblings was non-existent. The house was a little out of control. As far as being the man of the house, I didn't wield any power with my siblings. They just did what they pleased most times. Working was a little piece of quiet for me when the home was too loud.

When junior year comes close to an end, future plans start to be the topic of discussion. With college around the corner, the choices of where to go to school lurked in the background through the last year of high school.

I was still having thoughts of my love on the regular. Despite the temporary relief of not seeing her every day, the ache of her absence clawed at my soul. It hurt that she had found someone else. The thought stung like a fresh wound, a constant reminder of what could have been. Time appeared to slip through my fingers like sand, soaring by so swiftly that before I knew it, senior year had tiptoed onto the stage of my life.

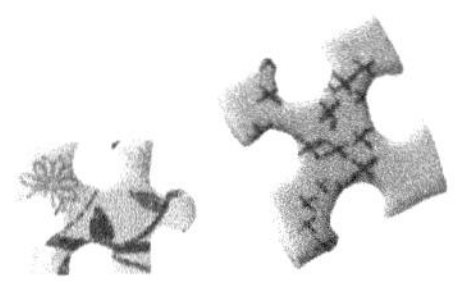

Chapter Eleven

Senior Year

Senior year carried with it a heavy weight—the pressure to decide what came next. Would college be an option for me? This question, though of monumental importance, had not been given much thought. Survival had been the sole focus. My early dismissal granted me respite, for I only had to take four classes. By noon, the school day was behind me.

One of those four classes, my last of the day, was Advanced Honors Typing. I excelled in this class, surpassing the curriculum for the entire year by the end of the first semester.

The thought of sharing a class with my heart's kryptonite terrified me. I wished for the same luck as the previous year, praying that we would have no classes together. Out of sight out of mind, right? My heart yearned for the pain to stay at bay.

Hope flickered within me as I navigated through my schedule, not catching a glimpse of her all day. Perhaps the universe had finally granted me a reprieve. How wrong I was. Just moments before the bell signaled the start of class, she walked in, a note in hand. She handed it to the teacher, who studied it briefly before motioning for her to take a seat. I couldn't believe my eyes. How had fate conspired to place us together again?

Reluctantly, we settled on opposite sides of the classroom, maintaining a distance that seemed prudent. It worked, for a while. We spent a week skirting around each other, careful not to let any conversation slip between us. And then, unexpectedly, the teacher made a decision that took the class by surprise. Frustrated with our constant whispering, he rearranged our seating in alphabetical order by last name.

As the teacher called out the names, I held my breath, hoping the veil of fate would continue to shield me. But destiny had other plans. I stood still, frozen, as my name was called. When the teacher announced her name, she too remained standing. With a sigh of resignation, the teacher directed us to sit next to each other. He believed my excellence could guide her, the weaker student.

Thus began our silent reconciliation after a year and a half of silence. We resorted to writing letters to each other, slipping notes beneath the keyboard, even though we were side by side. Talking out loud seemed too difficult, too raw. Our conversations danced across those papers, filling with all the words left unsaid, creating a connection that was both painful and necessary.

As senior year climaxed towards its closing act, an unlikely friendship blossomed. We grew to accept and understand each other in ways only time, maturity, and a shared history could forge. She remained with her boyfriend, and I carried the weight of my wounded heart. But in the end, we left behind the confines of high school as friends, our stories intertwined and our journey forever etched in our memories.

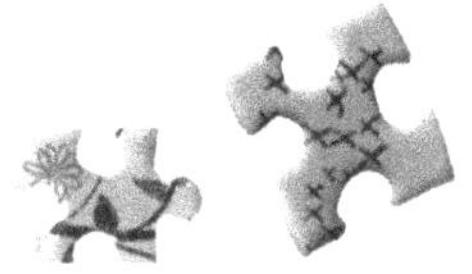

Chapter Twelve

At a Crossroads

After high school, I found myself at a crossroads. Not really knowing my value just yet, I had applied to over 24 colleges. To my astonishment, 23 of the 24 colleges had accepted me into their schools.

As the man of the house, I had always felt a responsibility to stay close to home and take care of my family. So I enrolled in community college and got a job at the mall, thinking it was the responsible thing to do.

After a while, I started feeling burnt out and suffocated by the familiar confines of my small town. Community college really felt like high school 2.0. I knew I needed a change, an escape from the mundane. And with that realization, I made the bold decision to leave my comfort zone and join the military.

The experience of boot camp was nothing short of a shock to the system. The military stripped us of our individuality and worked tirelessly to rebuild us into what they wanted us to be. Haircuts were uniform, clothes were identical, and even our manner of speaking was molded to fit their standards.

The drill instructors were relentless, pushing us to the limits of our physical and mental endurance. Many recruits cracked under the pressure. Unable to bear the weight of the grueling training, they would tap out and quit. The drill instructors would always say their job was to weed out the weak.

Boot camp was supposed to last for six to twelve weeks, but for me, it stretched out for a seemingly never-ending twenty-two weeks.

During my time in boot camp, I became close with five other recruits who shared my determination and drive. Together, we formed a bond and strived to keep each other motivated and positive. Our exceptional performance in training earned us positions of authority within our platoon.

Whenever a recruit failed to meet the expectations set by the drill instructors, they would accuse them of being on their "own program," deviating from the strict guidelines set by the government. In a lighthearted attempt to jest, the six of us adopted the acronym MOP, which stood for "My Own Program." It was our way of finding camaraderie amid the chaos.

One day, we stumbled upon a flaw in the system. When the drill instructors checked our mail, they would confiscate any contraband (candy, medication, money, or trinkets from home) and secure it in a foot locker. The code of the foot locker was known only to them and the platoon leaders. Weeks went by without anyone performing an inventory of the foot locker, and this realization sparked mischief in our minds.

Taking name tags and patches from the laundry room, we sewed them onto uniforms, forging an illusion of authority. We then pilfered the money that recruits received from their loved ones, meticulously keeping track of our transactions in a ledger. With our own funds, obtained through these shady means, we ventured out at night during our fire watch duties, visiting the store to purchase *Playboys*, chewing tobacco, and cigarettes. We even creating homemade wine by fermenting fruit from the chow hall.

Our secret operation became an open secret. We grew complacent, believing that we had outsmarted everyone. One of our group even went as far as scribbling the infamous "MOP" signature on each of our footlockers. Though we thought nothing of it at the time, our actions would soon come back to haunt us.

That fateful weekend, while we were writing letters home or attending church, we spotted a fellow recruit, who had once sought to join our clandestine club, walking into the drill instructor's office and shutting the door behind him. Within minutes, the door flew open, and an enraged drill instructor stormed out, his face flushed red with fury. Like a tempest unleashed, he stormed through the squad bay, flipping over every foot locker bearing the MOP insignia.

Summoning all six of us to his office, the drill instructor bellowed, accusing us of crimes that would land us in jail. As he berated us, I noticed my five cohorts trembling and tears welling in their eyes. At that moment, I stepped forward and told him that they had no involvement in the shenanigans; it was I alone who was responsible.

The drill instructor dismissed the other recruits back to clean up the mess left in his wake of chaos. Impressed by my leadership and bravery, he presented me with a choice: start boot camp anew, enduring another arduous journey, or face expulsion from the military.

There was only one answer for me. I wasn't about to give up. So, I opted to be recycled, to start from the beginning while my MOP comrades continued their journey towards graduation.

With one week left with my original platoon, I gathered my fellow recruits and assured them that I would be fine. I held onto my resilience, knowing that I would meet them again on the battlefield someday.

On our final night together, we performed our duties as normal. During the night, a two-man night watch would patrol the barracks and keep the weapons and soldiers safe. Refilling canteens with water for hydration was also one of the duties.

My friends woke me up. Seizing a perfect opportunity for revenge, I took the canteens and walked into the bulkhead. I filled the canteens of the recruit who had betrayed us with my own urine. We had to drink so much water to stay hydrated that our urine was crystal clear. It looked just like the water. I walked out the bulkhead and I placed the canteens at the end of his foot locker.

Every morning before we would start our day, we would line up at the foot of our racks and pound the two canteens of water to start the day off hydrated. Until we finished both canteens we were not allowed to move off of that spot. We had to hold both canteens empty over our heads till we were acknowledged then we could go about our morning routines.

If anything that was not part of the routine didn't happen, you would be taken to the quarter deck and punished with physical activities like pushups, sit ups, or jumping jacks.

That morning I got the satisfaction of watching him drink both canteens—every drop down the hatch. The look on his face as he was drinking, knowing that he was drinking urine but couldn't stop for fear of what wrath the drill instructor would unleash on him if he didn't finish both canteens. After he was done he ran into the bathroom to throw up.

Looking back I am not proud of my actions. I let my emotions get the best of me.

Later that week, I was sent to a new platoon, back to the beginning of boot camp. Surprisingly, this setback turned out to be a blessing in disguise. While the other recruits struggled to adapt, I already knew what to expect. I embodied the qualities of a model soldier, excelling in training, and graduated without further issues. I had finally become an official soldier, ready to serve my country.

I had learned firsthand the consequences of my actions, the importance of loyalty, and the resilience of the human spirit. As I stood tall, with the confidence of knowing how much I could push my mind and body through made me stronger than before, wearing the uniform of the military, I knew that I had discovered a world far beyond anything I could have imagined back at home.

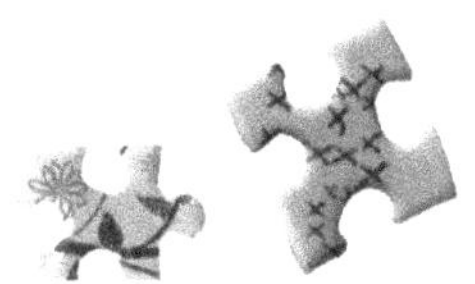

Chapter Thirteen

Military Journey

After completing boot camp, I was ready to embark on my military journey. Despite being a soldier, I still had to attend specialty school to fulfill my job requirements.

It was during my time at specialty school that I received an unexpected call from my mother. She informed me that a friend from high school had been searching for me. Reluctant to share my number, she instead gave her my address.

Although I didn't think much about it at the time, a week later I found a letter waiting for me in the mail. Intrigued, I promptly penned a response, providing my phone number. Soon enough, my special friend called, and our conversation flowed effortlessly as if we hadn't spent two years without speaking. It was a welcome reconnection.

When finished with specialty school, you got your orders to your first duty station base. They let you give a wish list of the three top bases you would like to go to and they would try to get you into one of those three. I graduated top of my class and was told that I would get my first choice.

Never believe what they tell you unless you get it in writing.

I had put down all east coast bases. The day we graduated is when we were told where to report for duty. When I got my orders, and they said Japan, I thought that they misread my request. I had said east coast, not far east coast!

Nonetheless, I was off to the Land of the Rising Sun for a year. After my year in Japan, I was stationed in Virginia, where the beach was just a ten-minute ride from the base. Every day after work, I found solace on the sandy shores, basking in the simple joys life had to offer.

But, as is often the case, when things seem to be going well, life has a way of reminding you of its unpredictability. Now that I was back home in the U.S., my mother came to visit me in Virginia. We hadn't seen each other in over a year. It was supposed to be a joyous occasion, a two-week vacation to reunite after over a year apart. The first few days were filled with laughter, beach trips, and shopping excursions. However, the sound of a ringing phone shattered our happiness.

It was news from home—my sister wasn't feeling well, and my mother's worry compelled her to cut her trip short and return home.

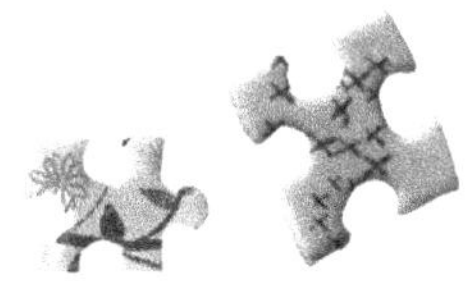

Chapter Fourteen

Intertwined Destinies

The following day, my mother called. It was urgent. She asked me to facilitate whatever was necessary for my return home. Arriving on a Wednesday afternoon, I was greeted with grim news. My sister had been admitted to the children's hospital, and her condition continued to deteriorate.

The doctors could do little beyond providing comfort. My mother couldn't bring herself to make the call and it fell to me to bear the weight of an agonizing decision. I informed the doctor that keeping her alive through machines wasn't what we wanted for her. It was time for her to find peace.

Having to handle a call like that would be tremendous for anyone. But it would have been so much worse for my mother to have had to make, after everything she did for us kids. There was no hesitation in my willingness to step up.

Tragedy, however, seemed relentless. On Friday, my mother's health took a turn for the worse, and she was admitted to the adult hospital across the street. Over the next two days, my brother and I found ourselves navigating a distressing journey between the hospitals, visiting our sister and mother separately.

As Monday morning arrived, we followed our usual routine and made our way to the hospitals. But this time, when I entered my mother's room, I knew something was amiss. Though she lay in her hospital bed, her attempts to speak resulted in only incoherent utterances bringing back feelings of my father's last few days on top of the gravity of what lay ahead. Overwhelmed, we decided to retreat to our home briefly. As we stepped inside, the phone began to ring insistently. I hurriedly answered the call, while my brother, sensing the gravity of the situation, anxiously awaited the news.

Before I could utter a single word, my brother glanced at me and asked, "Which one?" His eyes filled with dread. With a heavy heart, I revealed that it was our sister. She had passed away, and they needed me back at the hospital.

My brother decided against accompanying me. Understandably, he needed time to process the devastating news.

I returned to my sister's room alone, ready to undertake the painful task of tending to her lifeless body. As I approached her, I noticed her head turned to the left, as if she was looking but at what I had no answer at the moment.

As I moved to close her eyes, grief swirling within me, a nurse suddenly entered the room, tapping me on the shoulder and informing me of a phone call at the desk. With trembling hands, I answered, only to hear the voice on the other end declare, "Your mom just passed away. We need you next door." The dam of emotions burst free as I made my way across the street to my mother's bedside, tears streaming down my face in torrents.

As I entered the room, I approached my mother, silent and still, her gaze fixed to the right. It was as if she and my sister had already reunited, their souls recognizing that their time together had come to an end.

A painful realization struck me: my sister, born on my mother's birthday, departed this world on the same day. It was as if fate had always intended for their lives to be intertwined in this way.

The funeral, a day marked with unbearable sorrow, subjected my heart to its greatest tribulation. We laid them to rest side by side, their caskets interred in a twin grave. My mother found her final resting place with my sister, forever united in their bond that transcended the boundaries of life and death.

Since that heart-wrenching September, I find it impossible to revisit the graveyard. The memories are too potent, too tangible. It stands as a stark reminder of the immense loss I endured. But despite the pain that still lingers, I hold onto the strength found within their intertwined destinies, forever grateful for the love that defined their lives and touched my own.

That holiday season was the worst one I can remember, and no holiday has been the same since. The weight of responsibility fell heavily upon my shoulders as I returned home, knowing that my brother, still not yet 18, was now my sole responsibility. The house, the bills, and my brother's wellbeing all rested on me. Fortunately, the military understood the situation and assigned me to a temporary station at home with a reserve unit so that I could handle my affairs.

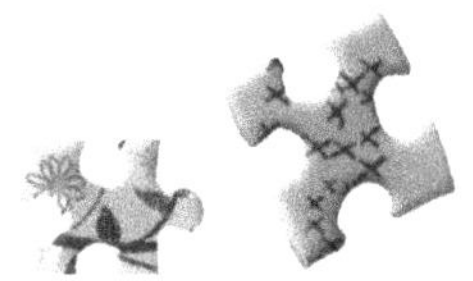

Chapter Fifteen

Special Friend

During this time, my special friend was nowhere to be seen. However, she had heard about what had happened to me, and a few weeks later, she reached out. It seemed like everyone knew about my struggles, yet she still chose to reconnect with me, just not during my darkest time. Our conversations flowed effortlessly, as if we had never spent any time apart. We even shared Christmas dinner with her family, and the warmth and acceptance I felt with them made me believe in the possibility of a serious relationship with her.

Filled with hope and excitement, I planned a grand New Year's Eve celebration at the casino. Just the two of us, creating memories together that would transcend that turbulent holiday season. But, as fate would have it, nothing went according to plan.

She invited her cousins and her cousin's boyfriend, shattering the intimate atmosphere I had envisioned. To make matters more complicated, one of her cousins was underage, preventing us from entering the casino. The night unraveled further as she spent a significant portion of it in the bathroom, overcome with illness. Adding to my disappointment, her ex interrupted our evening to wish her a happy New Year, shattering the magic of the night.

Despite the chaos and disappointment, I couldn't help but feel that this time with her was different. I was still floating on cloud nine, basking in the joy of having her back in my life. We continued to spend time together, talking and laughing, and for a month, I couldn't have been happier.

A few months later, she decided to go on a brief vacation to California with her cousin. I offered to take her to the airport. Before she left, I gave her a thoughtful gift and a card, hoping to convey my affection and wish her a good trip. As the week passed, I counted down the days until her return, excitement building with each passing moment.

Finally, the day arrived, and I picked her up from the airport, feeling an indescribable sense of joy and anticipation. As I dropped her off at her house, her mother kindly invited me inside, mentioning a mini party they were hosting. However, I declined the invitation, explaining that I needed to get some sleep before my work shift that night. Little did I know that this seemingly unremarkable farewell would mark the beginning of a two-year silence.

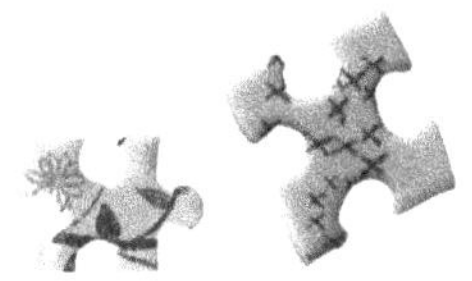

Chapter Sixteen

The Weight of Responsibility

Days turned into weeks, and weeks into months, with no sign or word from her. She disappeared from my life as abruptly as she had returned. Calls went unanswered, texts remained unread, and my heart sank deeper into a void of despair. This familiar feeling of emptiness, one that I had become all too acquainted with over the years, engulfed me once again.

As if facing the burden of the house, bills, and my troubled brother wasn't enough, this newfound heartache deepened my pain. My brother's alternative lifestyle, his recklessness, and his refusal to take responsibility for his own actions weighed heavily on my shoulders. Constantly surrounded by friends who encouraged him down a destructive path, he immersed himself in a world of excess and hedonism.

Despite all the challenges, I had made a promise to myself and to my mother that I would be there for him. Determined to keep my word, I had to make an impossible choice. The military, growing impatient, demanded my return to Virginia to resume my duties. But I couldn't abandon my brother and the life that needed my attention.

In the end, there was no choice. I made the difficult decision to leave the military, to stay home, and assume the burden of responsibility for my brother and the house. The future remained uncertain, with no guarantees of an easy path ahead. However, I accepted my fate with a heavy heart, knowing deep down that this sacrifice was necessary for the ones I loved.

The rest of that year and the next few years were a struggle for me, trying to keep the bills paid on time and looking after my brother. We continued to live in the house that we grew up in with our parents and sister, but it served as a constant reminder every day of what we no longer had in our lives.

Sometimes just walking into a room would bring up so many feelings that it would become paralyzing for a few seconds before I would be able to continue about my day.

Amidst the challenges, an unexpected phone call broke the monotony. It was from my special friend, someone I hadn't heard from in years. I answered, and as soon as I heard her voice, my heart skipped a beat. She began speaking, her words carrying a mix of regret and sorrow. She apologized for how she had treated me in the past and revealed that she had been diagnosed with cancer. She had moved in with her ex-boyfriend, the very person she had been with when we first met.

I was at a loss for words, unsure of how to respond. All I managed to say was that I was sorry too, then we hung up. After that call, the silence between us resumed, and I didn't hear from her for a while. There was so much else going on in my life at the time. I struggled to find a stable job, and the bills became increasingly difficult to keep up with. Money was running low, and I found myself fighting to save our family home as the bank threatened to take it away.

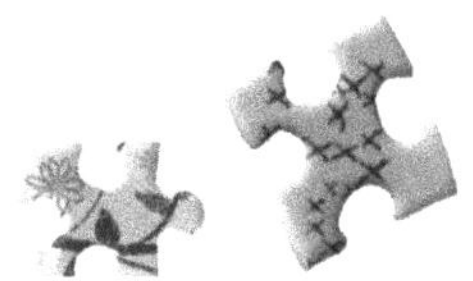

Chapter Seventeen

Security

Desperate for a chance to turn my life around, I seized an opportunity to work as a security guard at a local prestigious college. It felt like a fresh start, a glimmer of hope in the midst of my struggles. I embraced the night shift, juggling work with daytime classes, believing that things were finally falling into place.

But reality soon made itself known. The campus, located in the heart of the city, no fences to separate the campus from the city streets, became a hotspot for late-night robberies and assaults. Students, seeking drugs, often found themselves in dangerous situations. Every night, the security office was flooded with reports, and injured students recounting desperate attempts to score drugs.

In that chaos, an idea formed within me—if the students had a safe, reliable source for their drugs, it could potentially reduce the number of robberies and incidents we dealt with. Naively, I believed my plan wouldn't have any negative consequences.

Amidst my overwhelming schedule, I started a side business, needing a partner to help manage the growing demand.

As the business took off surprisingly fast, my life began spiraling. Balancing nights at work, days in class, and the demands of my newfound venture pushed me beyond my limits. The need for a supportive partner became evident, but finding one proved challenging.

Finally, I found a partner who seemed capable of easing some of my burdens. I discreetly dropped off the necessary supplies at his dorm room, strategically hidden within a bottomless flower pot. I had established a routine of restocking twice a week, confident that our discreet arrangements would go unnoticed.

But fate, once again, had different plans. One day, I received an unexpected call to restock at my partner's room. Unbeknownst to me, a small party was underway when I arrived. Oblivious, I entered and exited, convinced that I hadn't been seen. It turned out, however, that a freshman, who worked part-time in the security office, caught sight of our exchange.

The following Monday, he confronted me about the company I kept, expressing shock at what he had witnessed. He hinted at my partner's reputation as a known drug dealer on campus. In response, I claimed ignorance and attempted to brush off the situation as a misunderstanding, mentioning our shared class as an excuse for my presence.

Unfortunately, he took matters into his own hands and reported the incident to the director of security, expressing his concern. An internal investigation ensued, with a month's worth of information gathered before I was called in for a meeting.

Sitting in that room, I was faced with the weight of the allegations against me. Denying everything, I insisted it was all a misunderstanding. But my pleas fell on deaf ears. The director revealed that he had received 50 statements from students who claimed to have seen me participating in parties while on duty. His final words hit me like a sucker punch—I was being fired.

As I left the room, my mind raced with a mix of emotions—betrayal, disappointment, and regret. The dreams of stability and redemption I had glimpsed momentarily were shattered. The struggle to keep afloat continued, now stained with the bitter taste of lost opportunities and a tarnished reputation.

And so, the following years became a saga of resilience, a journey forged through hardship, lessons learned, and a fervent hope for a fresh start.

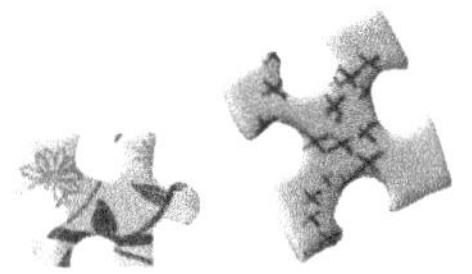

Chapter Eighteen

Rock Bottom

I had hit rock bottom in life, struggling to find decent work in a time when jobs were scarce. Desperation consumed me, pushing me towards a path I never thought I'd take. Selling drugs became my means of survival, even though it weighed heavily on my conscience. It was a necessary evil, the only way to keep the lights on and the relentless bill collectors at bay. My modest home became a revolving door of people, parties, and other bad life choices. Looking in the mirror, all I could see was a constant reminder of the life I wanted to leave behind.

Determined to turn my life around, I filled out countless job applications, willing to take on any manual labor job just to earn an honest living. Desperation was settling in and I was willing to take any job even if it was too good to be true.

One job like that presented itself to me. The ad in the news-paper read, "Looking for people who want to make over 50k managing stores. No experience necessary. Will train motivated individuals." I called the number and they told me to come to the place where they were doing interviews. I showed up and it was in a Holiday Inn conference room. There were over 30 people in the room.

Then something like an infomercial started. It was like one long sales pitch. It was run by twin brothers and their boss. The twins were the face of the company. They were who we saw every day and who we would interact with all the time. Their boss was a midget. He looked like the guy from the get-rich-quick scheme commercials that were on TV at 4 a.m. He was the closer, the charismatic one. He sold us desperate souls a pipe dream.

Well, for the next hour and a half I listened to their pitch and learned I would have to invest in the training ourselves. We had to purchase the starter kit for the training. It was 100 bucks and then on Monday we would start learning the business to be a manager.

Monday came and when I got to the office for training we were learning sales. It was selling fire safety equipment. The twins said that we had to sell first for them to learn how to manage our own store. I gave everything I had to this job as I saw it as a way out of the life I didn't want anymore.

After a month of working for the twins I noticed that the training wasn't progressing and then the checks started to bounce. Also my family and friends who had purchased materials from me weren't getting their orders.

Something wasn't right. A few of us employees tried to confront the twins the next week, but when we showed up, everything was gone. The twins had left and ran off. The job was a scam and we all got played. I felt like a fool and what was even worse was that my friends and family were played as well because of me.

That didn't end well but I couldn't let it stop me. I had to pick myself up and get back on the job hunt. Finally, a glimmer of hope emerged when a temp agency offered me a job at a warehouse, making decent money.

Less than a month later, an unexpected opportunity to advance to the warehouse manager position emerged, prompting me to apply. To my surprise, I got the job. As if the universe was showing me a glimpse of redemption, I also landed a part-time role in a middle school's afterschool program.

Days turned into a whirlwind as I left home at the crack of dawn and returned after dusk. The pieces of my life were slowly falling into place—bills were being paid, and my stomach was no longer constantly gnawing with hunger. One weekend, feeling the weight of my newfound responsibilities, I decided to unwind and drown my worries in alcohol. As I meandered around downtown, fate played a hand, leading me to encounter the brother of someone I held dear—my special friend.

He stood tall as a bouncer at the local club, and when our gaze connected, I couldn't help but unleash my emotions upon him. The alcohol-fueled ramblings spilled from my lips as I expressed how deeply I had loved his sister and how she had never given me a chance. Little did I know that he found my heartfelt outpouring amusing, and upon arriving home, he shared the entire tale with her.

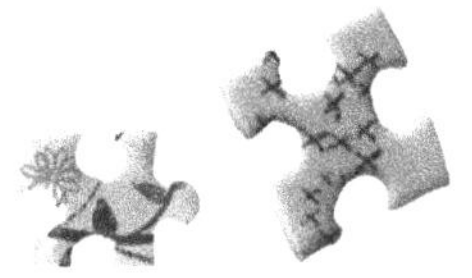

Chapter Nineteen
Engagement and Marriage

A phone call from her later that week revealed the mischievous game her brother had played. She recounted the story and admitted that my love-filled words had touched her deeply, leaving her unsure whether to reach out. We began to talk again, the easy flow of conversation making it feel as though we hadn't spent any time apart. Hope flickered within me as I wished that this might finally be the right time for us to be together.

Our relationship blossomed. We were spending every day talking and every other day hanging out. Our first date was watching a movie at my house. It was *Slow Burn,* a crime drama about firefighter investigators. All I remember was the movie being on replay over and over for almost six hours. The first hour we watched the movie, the other five hours we watched our tongues in each other's mouth.

Not long after that date, I was at the mall doing some shopping and I was walking past a jewelry store. Some voice in my head just said, *Stop and take a look. There is no harm in looking.*

So I walked in and there was a beautiful engagement ring just staring at me. I asked the clerk about the ring and it turned out that it was a custom-made ring for a customer who changed their mind and didn't want it anymore so there was a discount on the ring. None of that mattered to me. It was perfect.

I had to act fast so I put a down payment on the ring and walked out of the store feeling great!

We were now spending almost every day together and I didn't want the feeling to end, so I asked her about moving into my house. She wasn't surprised by the question and without hesitation she replied, "The only way I would move in is if you put a ring on it." She laughed.

I said just as fast, "Be careful what you ask for, it might already be in the works."

She didn't believe my comeback and called me out on what she thought was my bluff. We went down to the mall. I showed her the jewelry store that had the ring, but she didn't see the ring. Until she saw my account, I don't think she really thought that I had got a ring.

Less than a month after that visit I had paid off the ring and not before long, we found ourselves engaged and living together in my house.

However, life's sense of irony prevailed, and just when everything seemed to be falling perfectly into place, news of budget cuts at my warehouse job reached me. Regrettably, I was among the unfortunate few let go. Despite this setback, I couldn't fathom that my wishful thinking, endless hoping, and years of dreaming were finally becoming a tangible reality.

Our engagement lasted nearly a year before we ventured down the aisle. Even amidst the pressure and uncertainty surrounding my employment, our wedding felt like a seamless affair. The venue was perfect, and not a single issue disrupted our celebration. The excitement rippled through us as we embarked on a honeymoon in Mexico, creating memories like snorkeling, swimming with dolphins, and seeing the pyramid ruins that would last a lifetime.

However, the year leading up to our marriage proved tumultuous for me in terms of employment. I moved from job to job, counting five in total. Meanwhile, my wife remained steadfast in her commitment to the same company for nearly a decade. The weight of responsibility bore down upon me, exacerbating the pressure to secure a stable occupation. In a twist of fate, I found myself working as a security guard at a gentlemen's club, an ill-fitting setting for a married man.

As the pages of my story continued to unfold, I was left wondering if I would ever find my rightful place in the world, where I could stand tall and proud both as a husband and a provider. But deep within me, a spark of hope remained, promising that my journey was not yet over, and that there was still time to embrace a brighter future.

Chapter Twenty

Emptiness

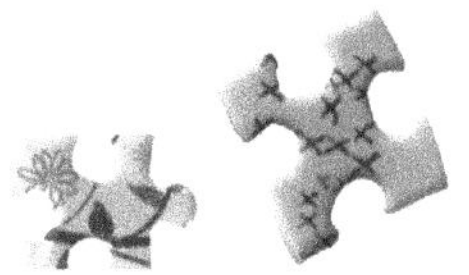

The first year of marriage, they say, is the honeymoon phase, where everything is happy-go-lucky. Those expectations had clouded my mind for so long that when reality failed to meet them, it sent me spiraling into a deep depression. I had longed for this marriage, fantasized about it, and built a vision in my mind of what it would be like. But the truth was far from what I had imagined.

I shut down, isolating myself from the world, keeping everything bottled up inside. My life wasn't ready for the commitment of marriage. I foolishly believed that being married would fix my underlying issues, but in reality, it only worsened my depression and made me an inadequate husband.

Simple day-to-day tasks around the house became overwhelming. I struggled to keep up with the maintenance and upkeep, haunted by the memories left behind by my family in the house I grew up in. Going into the basement to do laundry, I would cry thinking about how I would be down there lifting weights while my mom did the laundry and talked to me about life and school. I would be cutting the grass and go around the light pole that my dad put up in the back yard to give more light to the pool so we could swim at night. He was so proud that he put it up and wired it all by himself. Even just going to sleep, I would walk into my room that was once my mom and dad's room. I would just start to feel the presence of love and in an instant, it would be gone. I would feel that void again and just start to cry.

Getting up and going to start my day was a struggle. Most days I didn't want to get out of bed. The bills piled up, and I fought to get my life back on track. I had hoped that marriage would fill the void left by the absence of my own family, but I was wrong. The emptiness remained, and I failed to give my wife the attention she deserved.

Instead, I sought solace in my friends, who had become like family over the past fifteen years. They knew of all my struggles and were my pillars of support. But my wife saw my time with them as time spent away from her. While I immersed myself in my friendships, she dedicated her time to her own family—her father, mother, grandmother, brother, and sister. The space between us grew steadily, and intimacy faded away. I was married and yet felt utterly alone.

My depression reached an all-time high, fueled by the lack of quality time spent together. Working at the club only added to my inner turmoil. The constant presence of sexuality and intimacy made it increasingly difficult to resist temptation. To divert my wandering eyes, I delved into other destructive habits, encouraging the talent to find ways to make more money and supplying them with party favors for their work. The absence of physical intimacy in my marriage and the excessive time I spent at the club bred resentment and further fueled my depression.

I continued to isolate myself, while my wife sought solace in the company of her own family. As time passed, we found ourselves living together but growing further apart. The distance between us seemed insurmountable. Despite my efforts to distance myself from the club, the problems at home persisted. Night after night, I found myself sleeping alone on the couch, my snoring being the excuse that was driving an invisible wedge between us.

Eventually, I decided to leave the club behind and took a job at a group home for children. But even with this change, our problems at home continued. The couch became my lonely refuge, and my snoring remained an impenetrable barrier.

My time at the group home was short-lived, and the struggles in our relationship persisted. However, this story is not one of despair but rather a turning point. It's a tale of realization and redemption. It's the beginning of a new chapter, one where I was determined to heal the wounds in our marriage and to mend the broken threads that connect us.

Sometimes, it is through the darkest chapters that we find the strength to write a new story, one filled with understanding, growth, and the rekindling of love.

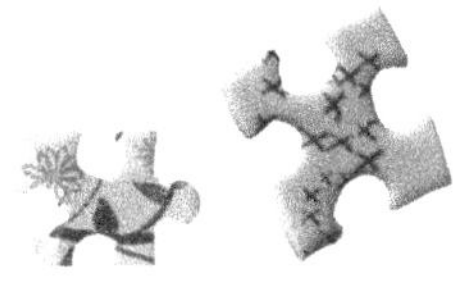

Chapter Twenty-One

Dreams Come True

I found myself in search of employment again. The constant hunt for a job can be discouraging, but fate intervened in the form of my coworker from the group home. He had recently left the group home to work with his brother at a local gym and, being the kind-hearted friend he was, offered me a job there. The pay wasn't impressive, but I knew that any form of income would help me through this tough period.

As I started my journey at the gym, my friend, who had been promoted to manager, became my mentor. While he may not have been the most skilled manager, he taught me everything he knew, making sure I would be able to navigate the challenges of the job. But the smooth sailing was short-lived. One day, the gym's corporate headquarters decided to relieve my friend of his managerial duties, deeming him unfit for the role.

With management changes often comes an overhaul in employee structure. I anticipated that everyone at the gym, including myself, would be interviewed and, most likely, dismissed. However, to my surprise, when the employees were questioned, they praised my abilities and relied on me to handle various issues that arose. Recognizing my capabilities, the corporation decided to give me the manager position and retain the existing staff. This unexpected turn of events filled me with hope for a better future, as it meant not only a raise but also the possibility of advancement within the company.

While my professional life seemed to be on the upswing, my marriage was struggling. Despite the challenges, my wife and I remained together, supporting each other through thick and thin. Lately, she had been feeling unwell, prompting her to visit a doctor because of her medical history. When she returned from her appointment, she came directly to the gym to see me. The moment she opened her mouth, my heart swelled with joy. She announced that we were expecting a child—a long-awaited dream come true.

Memories flooded my mind as I remembered the times we had sat in her grandmother's kitchen, imagining what our potential children would be like. Due to her having survived cancer twice we had to make sure that she was cancer-free for at least five years before we could even try to conceive a child. We had no guarantees that we would be successful, but now, that day had arrived.

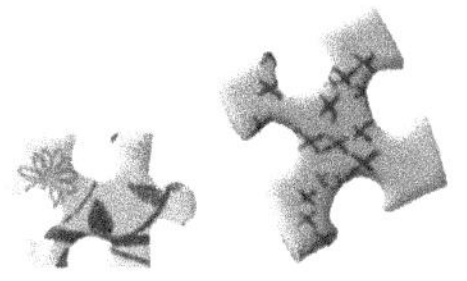

Chapter Twenty-Two

The Rhythm of Life

Together, we embarked on the journey of pregnancy, attending doctor's appointments and experiencing the exhilarating sound of our baby's heart beating. The rhythm of life pulsed through us, fueling our excitement. However, as we continued with our visits, the news turned sour. The doctor informed us that something was amiss—our child was not growing at the expected rate. Our hearts sank as we realized the magnitude of the situation. Our son, a cherished dream, was facing challenges before even entering this world.

Medical experts performed every test available, desperately seeking answers, but the results remained frustratingly inconclusive. Although the doctors suggested terminating the pregnancy, our unwavering love for our child made such a decision unthinkable. As the due date drew nearer, our son slipped further behind on the growth scale. With our baby's best interests at heart, the doctors recommended an early C-section to give him the optimal chance at survival. My son stopped growing at 23 weeks and at 32 weeks, my wife underwent the operation.

Our son made his entrance into the world, weighing a mere one pound six ounces. He literally fit in the palm of my hand!

The fragility of his tiny body amazed and humbled me. The doctor, cradling him gently, held him up to the light, just like in the iconic scene from *The Lion King*. And as they hurriedly whisked him away to the neonatal intensive care unit, my heart clutched in my chest. The following month was a tumultuous whirlwind as we balanced our time between the hospital and work. Every moment we could spare, we spent at our precious son's side, our love fiercely protecting him.

During this challenging period, my employment at the gym came to an end due to financial constraints. But fate, once again, intervened. A chance encounter with the manager of security at the children's hospital presented an opportunity to work there. I took the leap, leaving the gym behind, and a new chapter in my life began. The job aligned perfectly with my circumstances, located just ten minutes away from home and my son's medical appointments. It allowed me to attend every appointment while juggling the responsibilities of work.

As I settled into my new role within the hospital, I couldn't help but feel that this was where I was meant to be. My mother working there up until her passing and my sister being a patient there further tied me to this hospital. Life had bestowed upon me challenging circumstances, but it also guided me to opportunities that aligned with my aspirations and allowed me to be present for my son's journey towards health.

This poignant chapter in my life taught me the true meaning of resilience and the power of unwavering love in the face of adversity. As I continued to grow and evolve, my son mirrored my determination, proving that even the tiniest among us can hold immeasurable strength.

I loved my son with my whole heart, he was so small and yet he was the biggest deal in the world. From the moment he was born, I knew my life had changed forever. But as he grew older, it became evident that something was amiss. His growth was stunted, and despite numerous doctor appointments, we couldn't find a definitive answer.

The doctors attempted various treatments, from steroids to high-calorie diets, all in the hopes of kickstarting his growth. Yet, while my son did grow year after year, it was far from the rate of a typical child. Still, we remained determined to make his life better, ensuring he received therapy for his developmental issues at every turn.

It wasn't easy witnessing him struggle with his size while other children his age grew exponentially. I feared the day he would step foot into high school, where his kindness and small stature might make him an easy target for bullies. He also faced challenges in school, struggling to keep up with his peers, but once he understood something, he retained it with an unwavering grasp.

Now, nearly ten years old, my son's small frame remains a constant reminder of his uniqueness. But what he has lacked in physical stature, he has made up for in character. He is a remarkable child, funny and smart, with a memory that would make an elephant envious. And his heart? It is larger than life, overflowing with love and empathy for everyone he encounters.

Yet, amidst all our efforts to support our son, there were other battles we faced. My marriage, already burdened by the challenges that came with having a child with special needs, experienced difficulties with intimacy and communication. My wife often sought solace with her family instead of finding comfort at home with me.

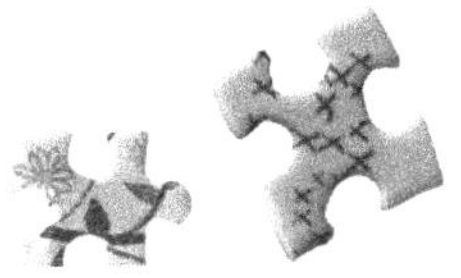

Chapter Twenty-Three
New Challenges

Life once again dealt me a blow. One day, my wife noticed something in my ear and asked if it hurt. I shrugged it off, thinking it was a harmless skin tag. However, a visit to the doctor unveiled a shocking truth—a rare form of bone cancer called spindle cell sarcoma lay hidden within me.

Thankfully, we caught it early, and the doctors successfully removed all traces of the cancer. They cut my ear open and removed all of the cancer, then took skin from my other ear to help fix the ear that had been cut open.

It was only a day procedure, but I've learned anything can happen and there's a risk even in small things. None of that came to pass and I became cancer-free, but my depression amplified. I gained an alarming amount of weight, tipping the scales at over 400 pounds.

Knowing I needed to make a change, I returned to the gym, eager to shed the excess weight and regain control of my health. However, working the night shift made it challenging to find time to exercise. Exhaustion often won over my desire for self-improvement. My wife recognized the strain I faced and insisted I see a sleep doctor.

At the sleep clinic, it was revealed I stopped breathing a staggering 100 times an hour during sleep. They prescribed a C-PAP machine, and it revolutionized my life. With improved sleep quality, energy coursed through me, and my moods brightened. The gym once again became a regular part of my routine, where I worked out two to three times a week.

But pushing myself led to new challenges. After an intense workout one day, I returned home and collapsed, feeling as though a massive boulder was crushing my chest. Concerned, I rushed to the emergency room, where a doctor delivered disturbing news—a six-mm-wide tear had developed in my aortic valve. The doctor compared my situation to that of a ticking time bomb inside me. At any moment it could go off and explode, ending my life.

Though the tear was monitored for nearly a year. I was working out five to six times a week trying to get in better shape to help my heart condition, but it began to expand, creating a fan-like pattern of danger. Emergency surgery became inevitable. Despite my anticipation of a positive checkup, the doctor delivered a sobering message, demanding immediate action.

As I prepared for yet another life-altering surgery, I reflected on the journey I had embarked upon. From my son's growth struggles to my battle with cancer and weight gain, life had thrown obstacle after obstacle in my path. But resilience pushed me forward, promising a brighter future.

I was under the knife less than four days after the doctor's visit. It was a necessary six-hour procedure, and then I spent two days confined in the intense grip of the intensive care unit. The days blurred together, and when I finally woke up in the hospital room, it felt as though I had been asleep for mere minutes rather than days. But the throbbing pain that coursed through my body harshly reminded me of the reality of the situation.

My muscles screamed in protest as I attempted to move. Every breath, every slight motion, brought a new wave of agony, a stark reminder of the extensive work that had been done to me. I was trapped, unable to walk, talk, or even take a breath without feeling the sting of pain coursing through my weakened body. The simplest acts had become monumental challenges.

For the next two days, I pushed myself relentlessly, trying to get my legs and other body parts back into action. The previous days had left me helpless, stripped of my independence and dignity. The loss of control over my bowels during the initial stages of recovery left me devastated, forced to experience the discomfort and embarrassment of going to the bathroom on myself. It was a humbling and frustrating experience, intensifying my feelings of helplessness.

But amidst the moments of despair, there was a flicker of determination within me. I was determined to get better and to regain control over my own body. The doctor's reassurance that I would be able to return home on Monday brought a glimmer of hope. Though still weak, I felt a surge of optimism as the days passed. My body was healing faster than expected.

By the fifth day, I felt a significant improvement. I could finally use the bathroom normally again, a small victory in the grand scheme of my recovery. I willed myself to stand, to walk, and slowly, with my own strength, I moved forward. Each step was a testament to my resilience and determination.

The hospital staff observed my progress in awe, and to their surprise, they discharged me two days earlier than planned. As I stepped out of the sterile hospital environment and into the warm embrace of home, a wave of relief washed over me. The day I returned home felt like a reunion with a long-lost lover, a gentle reminder of the comforts and familiarity that awaited me.

But as I settled into the sanctuary of my own space, I realized that my journey towards healing was far from over. The walls around me held echoes of the challenges I had faced, and the scars on my body told tales of resilience and perseverance. I knew the road ahead might still be arduous, but I was ready to embrace it with unwavering determination. The day I came home might have felt good, but it was just the beginning of my triumphant and transformative journey towards complete healing.

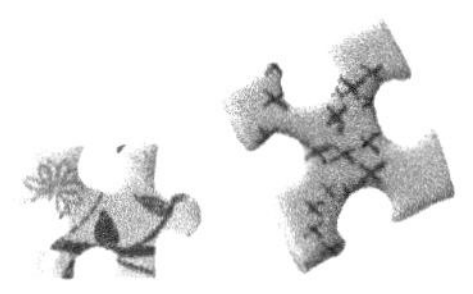

Chapter Twenty-Four
Sanctuary

The first week back home was a big adjustment. I had spent a week in the hospital, battling a serious heart condition. Finally, I was back where I belonged—in the comfort of my own home. But as I stepped over the threshold, an overwhelming feeling of discomfort washed over me, as if I had entered a completely foreign place.

The familiar hallway that once echoed with laughter and joy now seemed empty and devoid of life. The walls, once adorned with cherished family portraits, were now bare, and the rooms felt cold and unfamiliar. It was as if time had stood still, freezing my home in a state of abandonment.

But what unsettled me the most was the news that awaited me upon my arrival. While I was having my chest cracked open and my heart operated on, my car had been stolen right from my in-laws' driveway. It was later found, battered and totaled, abandoned on the side of a desolate road. The mere thought of someone violating my personal space, taking away something that had been a symbol of my freedom, left me with an unsettling sense of vulnerability.

As if fate was determined to test my resilience, my attempt to find solace in a hot shower was thwarted. The basement, a place usually reserved for storage and utilities, had become a victim of nature's wrath. Massive rainfalls over the past few days had caused the basement to flood, leaving me without hot water and exacerbating my already fragile state of mind.

As I stood in my once cozy living room, now stripped of its comforting warmth, I couldn't help but feel an overwhelming sense of displacement. I gazed out the window, searching for solace in the familiar sights of my neighborhood. But even the trees, once vibrant with life, seemed indifferent to my return, their leaves rustling in the wind as if whispering tales of my absence.

Determined to reclaim my sense of belonging, I decided to tackle one problem at a time. I contacted the insurance company about my stolen car, hoping for a small semblance of justice. I reached out to repair crews to fix the damage caused by the flooding, hoping to restore my home to its former state of comfort.

Hours on the phone on hold turned into days as I navigated an unfamiliar landscape of insurance claims, repair work, and emotional turmoil. Slowly but surely, the pieces of my life began to fall back into place. The insurance company settled my claim, providing me with the means to purchase a new car. The repair crews worked tirelessly to restore the basement, ensuring that hot water would once again flow through the pipes.

As the repairs wrapped up, I stood in my newly restored basement, marveling at the resilience of the human spirit. The once-drenched walls now stood firm, painted in warm hues that brought a sense of life back into the space. And as I ventured into the world with my new car, the wind in my hair and a renewed sense of gratitude in my heart, I realized that discomfort and adversity had transformed an empty house into a sanctuary of growth and strength.

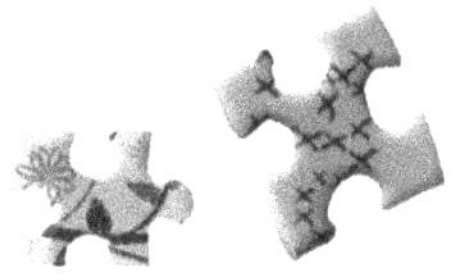

Chapter Twenty-Five
Through the Darkness

In the stillness of the night, the quiet hum of the house enveloped me as I sat in the recliner chair in the living room. The soft glow of the lamp beside me cast gentle shadows on the walls, creating a sense of serene solitude. It had been a few weeks since I had returned home, and the familiar creak of the stairs still echoed in my mind.

Each step up and down was a painful reminder of the recent operation that had left my body weary and my spirit longing for the comfort of my own bed. But for now, the recliner was a temporary sanctuary, a place where I could rest and find solace in the quiet darkness of the night.

The first night back home, I had braved the discomfort and attempted to sleep in my own bed. But the pain that washed over me was more intense than I had anticipated, forcing a retreat back to the reassuring embrace of the recliner. As I settled into the chair, I murmured to myself that it wasn't so bad, that I could endure a little more discomfort until I could once again lay my head on my own pillow.

The days passed in a blur of lingering soreness and diminishing pain medication. With no refills left, I had rationed the remaining pills, saving them for moments of unbearable anguish. My body seemed to rebel against the notion of healing, each twinge a stark reminder of the recent surgery that had left me vulnerable and achingly aware of my own mortality.

And then, in the dead of night, as I slept in the recliner, a sudden jolt ripped through the stillness. I awoke to a terrifying view of the ceiling swirling above me as the chair tipped precariously, sending me crashing to the ground. Panic gripped my heart as I realized my leg was trapped, wedged tightly between the chair leg rest and the unforgiving floor.

My body contorted awkwardly, the upper part of my body sliding down the sloped chair while my pinned leg remained firmly rooted in place. The sensation of being pulled in two different directions sent a wave of fear coursing through me, my cries for help ringing out in the silent darkness.

But my pleas fell on deaf ears as my wife slumbered peacefully upstairs, unaware of the turmoil unfolding below. The fresh wound on my chest throbbed with a fierce intensity, threatening to tear open as the struggles grew more desperate. Each breath became a laborious task, the weight of my predicament pressing down on me with suffocating force.

With a surge of determination born from sheer survival instinct, I clenched my chest tightly and focused on freeing myself. Using my one free leg, I pushed against the wall with all my might, inch by agonizing inch, until I managed to dislodge my trapped limb from its confined prison.

As the pressure on my body eased, I rolled off the chair and onto the floor, my movements slow and deliberate. Pain lanced through me with every motion, but I grit my teeth and crawled towards my cell phone, a lifeline in my time of need.

With trembling fingers, I dialed my wife's number, the urgency in my voice cutting through the stillness of the night. It took an eternity for her to make her way downstairs, but when she finally arrived, she found me on the floor face down battered but unbroken, proof of the strength that lay dormant within.

As she helped me to my feet, I realized with a newfound sense of clarity that I was stronger than I had ever imagined. The ordeal had tested my limits, pushing me to the brink of despair, but I had emerged from the darkness with a resolve that burned brightly within me.

With each step towards recovery, I carried the knowledge that I could not be stopped, that the journey ahead would be fraught with challenges but that I possessed the resilience to overcome them. And as I settled back into the recliner chair, the soft hum of the house enveloped me once more, a soothing balm for my weary soul. The night passed in quiet contemplation, a whisper of hope threading its way through the darkness, lighting the path towards a brighter tomorrow.

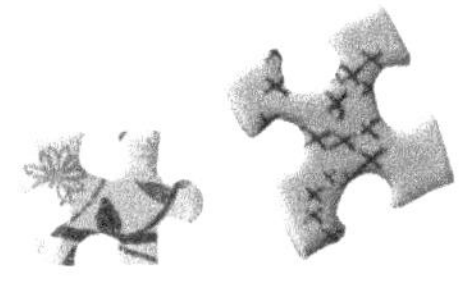

Chapter Twenty-Six

Stepping Back Into the World

Amidst the golden hues of a late summer afternoon, the hum of cicadas filled the air as I took my first hesitant steps back into a world I had temporarily left behind. For three long months, I had been cocooned in the safety and seclusion of my home, nursing both my physical and mental wounds. Each morning, I took a slow, deliberate walk around my neighborhood, the rhythm of his footsteps a soothing calm to my restless mind.

The first month was a test of patience and resilience. My body, once accustomed to the rigorous demands of the gym, now felt foreign and fragile. But I persisted, my determination unwavering, as I willed my muscles to remember the strength they once possessed. The simple act of walking became a ritual of self-discovery, a quiet meditation on healing and progress.

As the days stretched into weeks, my confidence began to blossom anew. The gym, with its gleaming machines and clanging weights, beckoned to me like an old friend. I approached my workouts with caution, testing the limits of my body's endurance, relishing the burn of tired muscles and the exhilaration of pushing myself beyond the comfort zone. By the third month, I was a regular presence at the gym, my routine was firmly established, and my physical strength was returning with each passing day.

As my body transformed, so too did my mind grapple with new uncertainties and fears. The impending return to work loomed on the horizon, a daunting prospect after months of solitude and introspection. I had grown accustomed to the solace of my own company, my thoughts undisturbed by the demands of a bustling workplace.

And then there was the night shift. The thought of plunging back into the rhythm of nocturnal life sent a shiver of apprehension down my spine. The transition from days spent in the sun to nights enveloped in darkness felt like a daunting leap into the unknown. How would my body adjust to the upheaval of my sleep patterns, the relentless pull of fatigue tugging at my senses?

It was not just the prospect of sleepless nights that troubled me. The shift in personnel added another layer of complexity to my return. The familiar faces I once knew had been replaced by strangers, their names and quirks a mystery waiting to be unraveled. I found myself adrift in a sea of unknowns, my confidence wavering as I navigated the uncharted territory of a changed workplace.

In the midst of this uncertainty, one truth remained steadfast in my mind: I needed answers. The only way to quell my fears and doubts was to confront them head-on, to step back into the world of work and unravel the mysteries that awaited me there. And so, with a mixture of trepidation and resolve, I made the decision to return to the familiar confines of my job, hoping that familiarity would breed comfort in the face of uncertainty.

Four months had passed since my return to work, and I found myself settled back into the night shift routine. The once-daunting prospect of nocturnal life had become a familiar rhythm, the darkness of night now a companion rather than a foe. My body, once fragile and uncertain, had regained its strength and vitality.

As I moved through the motions of my nightly routine, I reflected on the journey that had brought me to this point. The slow, steady progress of my physical recovery mirrored the gradual unfolding of my mental resilience. Each step, each lift, each shift served as a marker of my transformation, a demonstration of unwavering commitment to reclaiming my life and a sense of self.

I can close my eyes and see my family looking down from the heavens smiling at all that we have survived. I am still living in the same house with my son and wife. I know that my parents' sacrifice wasn't in vain. To see my son sleeping in the room that I slept in brings a warm feeling every time I walk into the room and kiss him good night.

Though I knew challenges still lay ahead, I faced them with a newfound sense of courage and determination.

The months of solitude and self-reflection had forged within me a resilience that could weather any storm, a strength that lay not just in my muscles but in the depths of my spirit.

As the night stretched before me, standing in the doorway with my wife watching our son sleep soundly in his bed, cloaked in shadows and filled with the promise of new beginnings, I knew that I was ready.

Ready to face the challenges. Ready to embrace the unknown. Ready to step boldly into the future that awaited me. I am stronger, wiser, and more determined than ever before to continue to build what my family started all those years ago: to leave their kids with a brighter future with the freedom to make it whatever they want it to be.

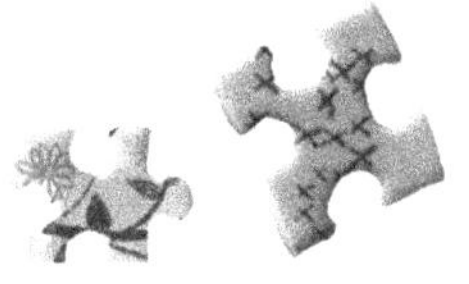

About the Author

Stephen Castro was born in the city that never sleeps—New York City—and raised amid the quieter rhythms of Connecticut. His journey is one of resilience, strength, and survival.

On the surface, his life looks like many others: happily married for 17 years, a devoted husband and father to a precious son who has his own struggles. But beneath this ordinary façade lies a lifetime marked by trauma and pain.

Stephen's story is proof that even when life shatters you into a thousand pieces, we can find the strength to rise again.

Faced with life's harshest lessons early on, Stephen found a fierce determination fueled by hope—for himself and his family. No matter how many times life tried to break him, he chose to stand up and rebuild. For anyone who has ever felt too broken to move forward, Stephen's journey offers hope—and the reminder that sometimes, the most beautiful stories are born from our deepest wounds.